Scriptures for t

Advent
2006

A Study Book

BOUND IN SWADDLING CLOTHES

Copyright © 2006 by Abingdon Press.

 **Abingdon Press**

All rights reserved. No part of this work may be reproduced or transmitted in any form or by any means, electronic or mechanical, including photocopying and recording, or by any information or retrieval system, except as may be expressly permitted in the 1976 Copyright Act or in writing from the publisher. Requests for permission should be addressed in writing to Permissions Office, P. O. Box 801, 201 Eighth Avenue, South, Nashville, Tennessee 37202-0801, or call (615) 749-6421.

Scripture quotations in this publication unless otherwise indicated, are from the New Revised Standard Version of the Bible, copyright © 1989 by the Division of Christian Education of the National Council of the Churches of Christ in the United States of America, and are used by permission. All rights reserved.

All readings taken from the Revised Common Lectionary © 1992 Consultation on Common Texts are used by permission.

ISBN ISBN 0-687-49765-5

Manufactured in the United States of America

06 07 08 09 10 11 12 13 14 15—10 9 8 7 6 5 4 3 2 1

Introduction

The Advent and Christmas seasons are so full of human activity that we can begin to think that all the "to-do" about the season is really about what *we* do.

We put up the decorations. *We* do the shopping. *We* do the cooking, cleaning, party planning, and wrapping of presents. *We* practice the Christmas cantata. *We* put our children in the Christmas pageant. *We* make the angel, shepherd, and sheep costumes that are required.

There is nothing wrong with doing all these things, but we run the risk of forgetting *why* we do them and letting *what* we do grab the center stage spotlight in our own little Christmas pageants.

The big "to-do" about the Advent and Christmas seasons is about *God's* activity, not ours. On center stage during each and every Advent/Christmas season is what God has done, is doing, and yet will do! We must be certain that what we do is *in response* to what is happening on the center stage where God is the star. We dare not try and steal the show!

As you participate in this study, I hope that the activity of God will stay in the spotlight and grab your attention. During the Advent and Christmas seasons, we are encouraged to take a special look at two great actions of God. One of those great actions is still ahead of us. God's love for creation is such that God, in the end, will not let evil have it. Christ Jesus will one day come in great power to reclaim this world for God's love and the kingdom of God.

The other great action for our focus is the birth of Jesus. Before God returns clothed in great power, God, out of great compassionate love, chose to come into this world bound in swaddling clothes. God's activity should always be on the center stage during the Advent and Christmas seasons.

A further hope for this study is that it will guide you in making a faithful response to the great actions of God that are the focus of the Advent and Christmas seasons. God's loving action demands a thoughtful response from us. We must not be careless with our activities but consider whether our longings—the gifts we seek to receive, the restoration we hope for, and the peace we desire—are worthy of the Love that came into this world bound in swaddling clothes.

Longings

Scriptures for Advent:
The First Sunday
Jeremiah 33:14-16
1 Thessalonians 3:9-13
Luke 21:25-36

Why does Christmas seem to take so long to get here? In our childhood, most of us experienced that mysterious stretching of time that occurs in the weeks before Christmas. A minute becomes an hour; an hour becomes a day; a day becomes a week. Only after a few years have been added to a child's age and the child has become an adult does the time before Christmas become a "quick" time rather than a "slow" time. What has changed?

For most of us, the intensity of our longing for Christmas diminished as we became adults. The added load of seasonal responsibilities (decorating, cleaning, preparing, shopping) is not something we greet with joyful anticipation. The pressure of our responsibilities seems to accelerate time to such a fast pace we have trouble keeping up.

What seemed to make the time before our childhood Christmases go so slowly was our longings for the magic of Christmas. How we enjoyed finding new gifts under the tree to unwrap! Now that we are older, we need to discover some deeper longings that the Advent and Christmas seasons can activate. The discovery of these deeper longings will slow back down the time before Christmas so that God can prepare us for the coming of a more profound Christmas gift—a gift bound in swaddling clothes.

Our longings can hold the key to our Advent season. If our longings are right, then we will be positioned rightly to receive God's Christmas Gift. If our longings are trivial, ill considered, or non-existent, we will not be in position to receive God's Christmas Gift when our souls wake up to Christmas Day. The lectionary Scriptures for the first Advent Sunday can help activate in us the right longings that will ready us for Christmas.

LONGINGS TO HAVE A PROMISE FULFILLED
JEREMIAH 33:14-16

"The days are surely coming, says the LORD, when I will fulfill the promise I made to the house of Israel and the house of Judah" (verse 14).

Children remember promises. A parent lets one promise slip out of the mouth, and a child will remember it forever. If it is a promise that the child delights in, they will not let the parent forget it. If it is a promise of punishment, the child will hope you forget it, notice if you do forget to punish, and then mark it down in her memory that mom or dad's threats are idle promises.

Children remember promises, but children often do not remember promises correctly. They can get a little confused by the details. A parent promises a child that *if* the child picks up the toys that are scattered throughout the room, *then* the child can go for a walk in the park.

Chilldren can also struggle with "selective memory," not remembering the *"if"* in the promise nor remembering the substance of what is promised. Without cleaning his room, the child can simply lock onto his version of the promise: "You promised me we could spend all day at the park, riding the rides, eating cotton candy, and swimming in the pool." The promise recalled is no longer the promise made by the parent; now it is the distorted promise of the child's selective memory.

The people of God must remember the promises of God. We are the children of Abraham, the ancestor of our faith, who walked with God because he believed the promises God had made to him (Romans 4). We, his spiritual children, keep moving through this life with our Lord because we long for God's promises to be fulfilled. In light of the importance of our longing for God's promises to be fulfilled, we need to make sure that we remember God's promises correctly. We do not want to fall victim to our often faulty, selective memory.

The people of God in Jeremiah's time had a memory of God's promise but not a correct memory. The people's memory of the promise and God's recollection of the promise were similar but not the same. It is not uncommon for the people of God to long for the promise of God to be fulfilled but to forget the "if" that accompanied the promise. When we forget the "if," we end up distorting the substance of the promise itself. When that happens, God's "promise" is no longer God's promise; it is a corrupted and distorted human substitute.

People are formed in the image of what they yearn for. If our longings are based on a distorted version of God's promise, we become distorted ourselves. For our own protection, God must speak from time to time the true version of God's promises. This is where prophets come into play. This was the task to which Jeremiah was called.

Jeremiah's prophetic task was large. The people he addressed in the name of the Lord were the people of God of the surviving kingdom of Judah. They longed deeply for the old promises of God to be fulfilled, but they did not remember the promise correctly. They had fallen prey to their "selective memory."

For one thing, they had forgotten the scope of God's promise. God's true promise included their exiled "ne'er-do-well" cousins of the northern kingdom of Israel, but many Judahites had come to think that God's promise was "just for them."

Some centuries before, the people of God had split into two kingdoms: the people of the southern kingdom of Judah, with its capital city of Jerusalem; and the people of the northern kingdom of Israel. There was often tension between the two parts of the people of God. The people of the Southern Kingdom had watched the destruction of the Northern Kingdom by Assyria in 722 B.C., perhaps with some understanding of how God could withdraw God's promise from such a reprobate and disappointing people.

On the other hand, the kingdom of Judah managed to survive. Therefore, the southerners may have assumed that God was still pleased with them. God would favor the deserving people of the Southern Kingdom by fulfilling God's promise, but God would forget God's promises to those rascals in the north. Jeremiah had to correct this faulty memory. He had to remind the people of the south that God still included in the promise the people of the north whom they were not particularly fond of (Jeremiah 33:14).

The people of God had also forgotten the "if" in the promise of God. The word remembered by the people was that God had promised them an unbroken line of kings from the house of David to sit on the throne. What the people of God had ill-remembered was that God's promise of a king in the line of David was conditioned by the heirs of David's line being devoted to God as King David had been.

Though God had shown great patience, God's patience can come to an end. They should not have expected God to sustain an eternal line of corrupt, unjust, and idolatrous rulers anymore than the modern people of God should expect God to sustain a corrupt government simply because it is "our" government. Babylon, serving as an instrument of God, was about to break the line of corrupt kings in Judah. In God's time, however, a righteous King from the lineage of David would eventually sit on the throne again (verse 15).

The people of God also had a faulty memory regarding the

security that God had promised. The people of God wrongly assumed that God would always preserve for them the safety and the freedom that comes with political autonomy. According to their memory of God's promise, no foreign power would ever take their freedom from them. They would always be God's people, safe and free.

Unfortunately, the people of God had forgotten the part of God's promise that addressed the righteousness demanded of the people of God. There could be no true safety or freedom apart from God's people practicing true righteousness. The tragedy was that not only had unrighteous kings embarrassed the name of God by feeding on the poor and needy and bowing to the gods of their own pleasure and corruptions, but a series of unrighteous kings had led the entire people of God down the path of unrighteousness.

Jeremiah lamented the damage caused by the unjust "shepherds" of the people of God. Kings were to be shepherds "after [God's] heart" who could lead the people in "knowledge and understanding" (3:15). Instead, the corrupted shepherds led the people astray. As a result, the people "forgot their own resting place" in the Lord and "sinned against the LORD, their true pasture," the Lord who sustained their lives (50:6-7, HOLY BIBLE, NEW INTERNATIONAL VERSION®). The people of God had become as unrighteous as their rulers, yet they claimed as their own the promises of God for safety and autonomy. How could God fulfill the dreams of peace while unrighteousness dwelled in the hearts of God's people? Unrighteousness destroys all true peace.

In restating the true promise of God, Jeremiah attempted to bend the people to the Lord's call on their lives. Jeremiah corrected their faulty memory by reminding them that God's promise is for the entire people of God, not just for a few. He reminded them that because God remembered the people of the Northern Kingdom, they should remember their cousins in the north as well.

When Jeremiah reminded the people that God would bring forth a righteous king, one who would "execute justice and righteousness in the land" (33:15), the reminder recalled the correlation between the righteousness of the leadership and the spiritual progress of the people. Because God does not ignore this correlation, the people of God should not be so naive as to think that the corruption of leadership carries no effect. The people of God must insist on right and just leadership.

In the last verses of the passage, Jeremiah reminded the people of God of the nature of the promise to them. God's promise of safety and political autonomy cannot be fulfilled outside of God's call to righteousness. At the heart of God's promise is God's dream for a people who may accurately be named "The LORD is our righteousness" (verse 16). Those who long for the promise of God to be fulfilled must not have longings only for safety and freedom. They must also long to be a righteous people.

Throughout this Advent season, as our longings grow for the gracious promises of God to be fulfilled, let us make sure that we remember the promises of God rightly. Our longings for well-being must include the heartfelt desire that others, too, might thrive in the peace of God. We must long for leaders in the church and in the nation who will serve God's just dream for humankind. We also must find in God's promise a deep longing for our lives to be so based in God's love and care that everything about us points to "the LORD is our righteousness."

In this Advent season, what promise of God do you long to be fulfilled?

How would you put into words the promise of God for your life at this time?

What is the role of righteousness in the promise you are awaiting? Who is the promise for?

What are the "ifs" to be reckoned with in the fulfillment of the promise of God you are longing for?

LONGING TO GATHER
1 THESSALONIANS 3:9-13

We often long to be with our family and friends during the Advent and Christmas seasons. Christmas is usually not a time that we choose to celebrate alone. Thus, our longing to be present at a gathering of loved ones at Christmas can be intense. Reading the passage from 1 Thessalonians, we encounter a longing to gather with brothers and sisters in Christ. This is an intense longing for a different kind of "gathering" that ought to be an expectation for our Christmas celebration, too. This Scripture passage can help us explore this unique form of gathering and increase our longing for it.

One of the section headings in our worship bulletin at church is entitled "The Gathering." In that section of our worship, we sing an opening hymn or two and often affirm our faith through the use of a creed. It was the leader of a workshop on worship who first introduced me to the term *gathering*. Prior to that workshop, gathering never had a religious meaning for me. After seeing the term used repeatedly in our worship bulletin, gathering means a lot more to me now. In fact, I now have a longing for it.

When the people of God gather, there is more going on than simply a group of people filtering into a church sanctuary. *Gathering*, in this religious context, refers to the people of God coming together around Christ. That is why in our worship bulletin "The Gathering" happens only after each of us is already in the sanctuary. "The Gathering" begins with a hymn that puts Christ in the center of our attention. "The Gathering" then continues as we affirm through a creed the Christ that is the ground for our common life as a church. It is not so much that we gather *in* a sanctuary; rather, we gather *with* the people of God and we gather *around* Christ. During this Advent and Christmas season, are you longing to gather with your church family around the One who was bound in swaddling clothes?

If you long to gather with your brothers and sisters in Christ this season, begin praying for your gathering family in Christ now. Because Paul longed to gather with his family in the Lord at Thessalonica, he began to pray for that family while he was still a long way off. Paul wrote this letter while quite a distance from Thessalonica and at a time when he was still uncertain of whether the Lord's travel plans for him would include another face-to-face encounter with the church at Thessalonica.

However, even the possibility of a gathering caused Paul to pray in earnest for the people. Paul's prayers were intense. When he prayed for people, it was as if he gathered them up with gratitude and they traveled together before the throne of God to find joyful fellowship with each other (verses 9-10). The gathering had already begun, in prayer, well before the longed-for gathering in person had yet to occur. Any gatherings we have with our church this season need to be saturated with intense, expectant, loving, and joyous prayer.

Paul's longing for a gathering with his people was also driven by godly purpose. Paul desired to be with the people of God in Thessalonica because he wanted—along with his companions—to "restore whatever is lacking in your faith." Travel in the age that Paul lived was doable but never easy. Merchants traveled extensively along Roman roads, but the incentive for merchants was the money that could be made. Paul did not share that incentive. Paul was known to work at repairing tents and other minor trades to avoid having to be supported by congregations that he was serving. When Paul did collect money, often it was to support his brothers and sisters in Christ who were struggling to eat.

So why did Paul travel so extensively along these ancient roads? Paul wanted to reach others with the message of Christ and build up the faith of those who were already believers. This was the purpose to which he was called. Traveling so far to gather with other Christians would not be worth the trouble if the gathering of Christians did not produce more faithful Christians.

We may never know what was lacking in the faith of the Christians in Thessalonica that could be restored through a gathering with Paul and his companions; but we do know that Paul wrote in Galatians 5:6, "The only thing that counts is faith working through love." Perhaps a gathering would have been of value to the Christians in Thessalonica if the gathering encouraged those Christians to love others as completely as Christ loved them. Our seasonal gatherings with fellow Christians should enable us to become more faithful and loving Christians. If they do not, of what ultimate value are they?

We present-day Christians could certainly use some Paul-like prayers sent our way at Christmas, particularly his prayer that "the Lord [would] make your love increase and overflow for each other and for everyone else" (1 Thessalonians 3:12, NIV). This prayer supports us in our mission during the Christmas season of gatherings. We never know whom the Lord might send to our churches during the Advent and Christmas season.

Persons unfamiliar to us often attend a Christmas Eve candlelight service, which many churches find to be the most highly attended service of the year, next to Easter. These "strangers" have come to gather *with* us and *around* Christ. God has entrusted us with their attendance! Will they be disappointed? They will not be disappointed if they encounter the love of the One bound in swaddling clothes. To prepare for such times of gathering during Christmas, we who seek to express the love of Christ must "increase and abound in love for one another and for all" (verse 12). We could use some prayer help to receive these seekers with love.

Finally, in this passage, Paul pointed to another gathering that the people of God long for. Paul included a prayer of preparation for that great day of gathering that is at the end of time. His assumption is that the Christians at Thessalonica would like to be numbered among the holy ones or "saints" of God.

None of us who know ourselves well are comfortable describing ourselves as being perfect in God's ways of love. Nevertheless, we are able to imagine the kind of work God desires to perform with us and through us. God can "strengthen [our] hearts in holiness" (verse 13) to a degree that far surpasses our view of ourselves.

It is not so much that we dream to be blameless before our Lord, but we do want to be numbered with our brothers and sisters who have a heart for Christ at the "coming of our Lord Jesus with all his saints" (verse 13). We do long for that last gathering time when we will all be washed clean of our sin, redeemed in love, and find ourselves enjoying the joy of the Lord together. The surprise is that when our longing for this final day of gathering takes root in us, we often find ourselves being so changed by the anticipation of that great gathering that we cannot help but enjoy our little gatherings even now.

Will the gatherings that you experience this season be truly valuable? Why or why not?

How prepared are you to love those that God sends to you during this season of gatherings?

How does longing for the final great gathering affect the way you live now?

LONGING FOR THE KINGDOM (WITH SOME APPREHENSION) LUKE 21:25-36

A new world is coming called the kingdom of God! If we were to paint a picture of this new world, at the center of the picture would be Christ establishing God's rule on the whole landscape. The effect of this rule would be peace, portrayed in the picture with a wolf living with a lamb, a leopard lying down with a goat, and a little child walking a calf, a lion, and a yearling on a leash (Isaiah 11:6). Obviously, when the kingdom of God arrives, it will not look much like our present world.

For heavenly peace to exist in this old world we live in, some cataclysmic changes are going to have to take place! While we can enjoy the thought of living in a "peaceable Kingdom," it is the thought of living on an earth that is going through the necessary cataclysmic changes that produces apprehension. "People will faint from fear and foreboding of what is coming upon the world" (verse 26). The kingdom of God we long for will not come easily. If you long for heaven on earth, you had best get ready to live through hell.

If we have experienced God's redemption in a significant way, we are familiar with what it feels like to surrender a treasured dream or cast off a judgment we were certain of. We know what it is like to have the coping mechanisms on which we have depended taken away from us. It hurts so bad it feels like "hell." Yet God must often take away, knock down, or destroy something of what lies inside us in order to make room for what God wants to bring to us. The end result of God's work is peace, but the process that brings peace is anything but peaceful.

After my first assignment as a pastor in The United Methodist Church, my wife and I took a leave of absence to spend a year in a Christian community. The community consisted of a network of homes bound by a common view of the Christian faith and a common practice of the Christian life. My wife and I entered this community because we longed for a new life in Christ. This longing was a form of a dream for God's kingdom. We wanted to walk in it!

What I did not realize is that for me to live a life more aligned with God's kingdom would require some catastrophic changes in what I thought to be true. What I valued, what I dreamed of, and how I went about getting by in this world were about to be challenged.

In one intense week, I finally had to acknowledge the changes that would be required of me if I were to live the "Kingdom" way.

I was so apprehensive about the changing landscape before me that I literally shook for two days. When I finally made the decision to walk into God's kingdom with God, peace came. Before I could walk in a little part of heaven, however, I had to make my way through a fear-filled hell.

What is true of God's work on a personal scale is also true of God's work on a large scale. The changes required of a sinful humanity and of a sinful human society to make room for God's kingdom are just too great for the changes to come peacefully. The arrival of God brings in its train disturbances that cause great apprehension.

Christ Jesus expects to find in God's people a deep longing for the kingdom of God. Because we are also a people of the earth, Christ is not surprised to find in us some apprehension about the coming changes as well. For the kingdom of God to be on earth, much must be taken away, knocked down, or destroyed.

This part of God's loving work is often called *judgment* in the Bible. Judgment is not a peaceful process; but it brings peace, and it always serves God's love. We need not fear the changes that God will work in us and throughout the world.

Others may look at the changes demanded by the loving judgment of God and take them as signs of a coming terror. We who know Christ see the cataclysmic changes spawned by God's loving judgment and receive them as preparations for a coming peace.

When we see the signs, we are told to "stand up and raise your heads, because your redemption is drawing near" (verse 28). Our longing to live in God's kingdom should never be diminished because of a growing fear of living in a world that is undergoing God's judgment. We have to go through the judgment to get to the Kingdom.

We also need to rejoice that the kingdom of God is well on its way. With the birth of a babe bound in swaddling clothes, God is with us, already establishing God's kingdom. God's rule is springing forth from God's grace and forgiveness, which was activated in this world by the redemptive work of Christ on the cross. Christ Jesus has been a seed of the kingdom of God, planted in the ground of a tomb, and now producing many seeds as Christ rules the hearts of believers (John 12:24).

All around us we expect to see evidence of God's work to establish God's rule. The evidence may be signs of peace that encourage us. The evidence may also be signs of judgment that cause apprehension. Either way, they are signs of God's power and glory at work in the world to bring in the kingdom of God.

With all of this work of God going on in the world, we had better keep ourselves up on our tippytoes, ready to see where God is working. Just as a construction worker needs to be watchful while among the dangers of a construction zone, we need to be alert and watchful. "Be on guard so that your hearts are not weighed down with dissipation and drunkenness and the worries of this life, and that day catch you unexpectedly, like a trap. . . . Be alert at all times" (Luke 21:34-36).

We cannot afford to have our minds preoccupied with lesser things while God is working God's wonders. If we are discerning of God's work, we will know when it is time to pick up a hammer, stand with God, and join God in building something God is making. We will also know when to step back and get away from something that God is tearing down.

As you long for the kingdom of God, what signs do you see of God's work to establish it?

What is your attitude toward God's judgment?

How great is your longing for the Kingdom even though the changes the Kingdom brings are disturbing?

Gifts

Scriptures for Advent:
The Second Sunday
Malachi 3:1-4
Philippians 1:3-11
Luke 3:1-6

For a child, pondering the gifts that might come at Christmas is often the predominant activity of the weeks of December. Thinking about the gifts that might make it under the tree can fill most of the waking (and many of the sleeping!) moments of the Advent season.

My dad was a representative for Gamble's Department Store. Each year in late November, he would bring home the Gamble's gift catalog and give it to his five children. For me, that catalog launched the Advent and Christmas season. Christmas was now so close that I would start to ponder and dream about it.

My sister and I would sit down with the catalog and play a game in which we imagined that we were each entitled to receive two gifts of our own choosing from each page in the catalog. With each page turned, our imaginary stockpile of Christmas gifts mounted towards the ceiling, each one added with an "Ooooo" or an "Ahhhh." We would play this game for hours as the thoughts of the gifts we might receive at Christmas filled the weeks to come.

We knew, of course, that out of all the gifts in our imaginary stockpile, only one or two might actually find their way to the base of the Christmas tree. Yet we continued to ponder the catalog, our choices, and the gifts that could greet us on Christmas Day. This exercise of imagination was worth every moment I spent due to the fun and excitement it engendered, the intimacy gained playing the game with a beloved sister, and the practice gained in the fine art of sorting and clarifying wants and desires. It is not necessarily a bad thing for children to ponder the gifts that come with Christmas Day.

Likewise, pondering the gifts that come with Christmas can be a worthwhile activity of the Advent season for adults, too. Each Scripture reading for the second Sunday of Advent points to a gift that shows up beside the manger of the One bound in swaddling clothes.

The gifts presented in each Scripture reading are gifts not common to a Christmas catalog but are worthy of our pondering. To ponder these gifts helps us sort and clarify our deepest desires; and, if we ponder these gifts in the company of other believers, an intimacy in the Spirit will result. In Malachi 3:1-4, we will ponder the gift of soap. Philippians 1:3-11 will encourage us to ponder the gift of partners. Based on Luke 3:1-6, we will contemplate the gift of a choice.

THE GIFT OF SOAP
MALACHI 3:1-4

During my junior high years, I found an unexpected gift in my Christmas stocking. The box was the right size to contain a watch, which I truly wanted. When I opened the beautifully wrapped package, however, what dropped into my hand was an Avon product called Soap-on-a-Rope. I don't know about you, but soap was not a gift I remembered asking for on my teenaged Christmas wish list!

Though not at all thrilled about the gift at first (How do you say thanks while holding a bar of soap as you pose for the camera?), I soon discovered the benefits of this utilitarian treasure. Soap-on-a-Rope was a useful tool for those who wanted to be clean (a concern of a young teenager with a growing interest in the opposite sex). The soap, hanging on its rope right in front of you when you showered, was always where it was supposed to be. When my first Soap-on-a-Rope disappeared with use, I wanted another one. I quickly decided the soap was not such a bad Christmas gift after all.

The Malachi reading for this second Sunday of Advent has us pondering the Christmas gift of soap. "But who can endure the day of his coming? Who can stand when he appears? For he will be like a refiner's fire or a launderer's soap" (verse 2, NIV). Do we really want to receive launderer's soap as a Christmas gift this year?

Malachi addressed a people who were expecting a different kind of gift from their God than a refiner's fire or a launderer's soap. Malachi spoke to the people of God around 450 B.C., long after their return from exile in Babylon to the ruins of their ancestral home. While thankful for God's gift of miraculous liberation from Babylonian captivity, the people had expected that their God would by now have created for them a bountiful and blessed life in the reclaimed Promised Land. They expected that the God who had acted so justly and powerfully in releasing them from Babylon would greet them in their home-land, dwell with them there, and bring great gifts of restoration.

Some of the gifts they expected were the restoration of the bound-aries and glory of the former kingdom; the restoration of the Temple and the priestly service to its earlier place of prominence; the restoration of the prestige of the Davidic line of kingship; and the restoration of the land to its former productivity and bounty.

However, the returning people of God found the conditions in the abandoned land so harsh that great effort was required simply to scratch out the barest necessities for life. They faced dry weather; irate neighbors; and ruined walls, buildings, vineyards, and fields. Long gone was the expectation of a quick and easy restoration. Now on center stage were the questions "Where is God?" and "Where are the gifts of God's blessing?" The questions strike at the core of the faith of the people of God.

Forms of those same questions still take center stage in the spiritual life of many. Some ask the questions as they survey the difficulty they are facing or as they look at the hard conditions of disease, poverty, hunger, war and injustice in our world. "Where is God?" "Where are the gifts of God's blessing?" In this Advent/Christmas season of expectation, there are persons who harbor a not-so-hidden despair: They have little real hope for an encounter with an active and loving God who will arrive in this world with good gifts in hand.

In answer to the despair and disappointment of the people of God in the day of Malachi, the prophet announced that God was indeed coming to God's people; but when God came, the gift God would bring would be a surprising one. God would arrive with the gift of soap! The people of God needed a thorough washing before restoration of any sort could take place. If restoration were to come, a bath would have to happen first.

The people of God were not sure whether the announcement of the advent of a soap-bearing God was good news or bad news! Not everyone delights in the announcement "Bath Time!" As a child, I did not enjoy taking a bath. In my judgment, taking a bath was a waste of time because I could see no need for it. To my way of thinking, "If I don't see any dirt, I'm not dirty enough to take a bath."

The people of God in the day of Malachi could not see the dirt that indicated their need to be washed clean. The prophet had a different perspective, however. "But who can endure the day of his coming, and who can stand when he appears?" (verse 2). The cleansing the people of God will receive when God comes with soap will be an exhaustive one. It will not be a sponge bath that cleans only the surface. It will be a real "scrub-down" affair that penetrates to the marrow and bone of our sin. It will be a holy cleansing that prepares us who have been set apart to begin to live fully God's life and service.

When Malachi addressed the people's need for a bath, he did not speak to their offenses against the grand biblical theme of justice or their participation in the spirit-deadening sin of idolatry. Instead, Malachi spoke of matters that many are apt to think are of far less importance. Malachi spoke of bringing poor quality meat to the altar of sacrifice (1:7-14). He mentioned marrying persons who were not people of the covenant (2:11-12). He spoke of too many among the people of God getting divorces (2:14-15) and of failing to tithe (3:8-10).

Do the presence of these offenses indicate a need for a sponge bath to wash the dirt off the surface of the skin, or do they indicate a soiled condition at the heart of people that needs deep cleaning? Malachi indicated that these offenses are not trivial matters; they strike at the heart of the covenant between God and the people of God.

How can we honor the importance of our relationship with God if we only try to get by "on the cheap" in what we offer God in sacrifice? How can we immerse ourselves in covenant living if we bind ourselves to unholy or secular ways of living? How can we honor our covenant with God if we break commitments we have made to others in God's name? How can we trust God to provide for our needs when we are too fearful to give a tenth of our income to God as commanded by the Lord? We need a thorough scrubbing!

Whether or not the words of the prophet help us see our need for a bath, the sight of One bound in swaddling clothes can show us our need. I am the father of two children. With each birth, I was humbled with a sense of unworthiness. "Who am I to deserve such a love-gift from Heaven as this? Beyond that, who am I to be entrusted to raise this precious gift?" That is when reality hit. "If I am going to be a good father, I will have to become a better man!" I became instantly aware that who I was was not enough for the task before me. I needed God's love to cleanse me, mold me, guide me, and enable me to do the love-task of raising children.

At Christmastime, we catch sight of One bound in swaddling clothes. This is the Holy One, the God of the covenant who has come to dwell with us. The love we see before us humbles us. Who are we to receive such a heavenly Love Gift? Then we are reminded of a task before us. We are to love in the name of this God who will restore this world with love. If we are to serve this God of the covenant in a ministry of reconciliation and restoration, we will have to become better men and women. We will need God to cleanse us, mold us, guide us, and enable us.

At first, launderer's soap may not seem like much of a Christmas gift; but I am convinced that most of us hunger to be cleansed by the Lord. We are tired of our dirtied lives and soiled hearts that prevent us from loving God and others the way God created us to do. We yearn to be a holy nation (1 Peter 2:9), but our lives are stained. We yearn to "declare the praises" (1 Peter 2:9, NIV) of him who redeemed us, but we do not look redeemed. We dream of the time when we will come before our God, offer the life we have lived on this earth as a tribute to God's honor, and find our gift "pleasing to the Lord" (Malachi 3:4).

However, these deep yearnings and our dream cannot come to pass unless we take a bath with God's launderer's soap. There is no other soap that can wash us clean. God's holy presence is the launderer's soap that can cleanse us of all unrighteousness. Look for the gift of soap this Christmas. It is just what we need!

What do you see as you look at God's people today that suggests God's people may need the gift of launderer's soap?

In regard to your life, to what would you like to see God's launderer's soap applied?

THE GIFT OF PARTNERSHIP
PHILIPPIANS 1:3-11

"In all my prayers for all of you, I always pray with joy because of your partnership in the gospel from the first day until now" (Philippians 1: 4-5, NIV).

Tennis partners, dance partners, business partners, bridge partners, partners in crime—our lives are marked with partnerships of all kinds. Each partnership is a unique mixture of joy, disappointment, comfort, frustration, elation, pride, sadness, success or failure that it funnels into our lives.

I can experience the whole gamut of these effects brought by partnership in one outing with a doubles tennis partner. Having just gone through a roller coaster of good and bad feelings with my partner, when we walk off the court in victory, I am ready to conquer my office work. If we lose, however, I suddenly feel depleted and worn out and have little interest in the other tasks that now await me. My tennis partnership can affect my life off the tennis court, but only for a short while. For good or ill, however, the effects of other partnerships can be more enduring.

Our more significant partnerships can be like unwrapped onions in the refrigerator: They add their distinctive flavors to every other aspect of our lives.

My grandfather was an adopted child. To be considered an equal partner in his adopted family name, my grandfather felt he needed to be as successful in making money as the uncles, cousins, brothers, and sisters who surrounded him. They seemed to flourish in making money, and he set out to flourish in that endeavor as well.

As a young man, he entered a business partnership in the purchase and operation of a car dealership.

He and his partner made the business work, and the money was coming in. Then the business partner disappeared one night after emptying the business accounts, leaving my grandfather with nothing but debts. The stench of this partnership worked its way into my grandfather, flavoring him for a lifetime.

Unable to cope with the distaste of a partner's betrayal and now tortured with questions of his own value in the light of such a colossal business failure, my grandfather sought relief through self-medication. My grandfather became a problem-drinker and then an alcoholic. My grandfather found liberation from alcohol later in life, but I still wonder if his self-esteem ever recovered from that bad business partnership.

The smell of that partnership flavored my grandfather's views of himself with a bitter taste. It also flavored my grandfather's view of the world with suspicion. As a consequence, the other significant partnerships of my grandfather's life (such as his marriage) felt the effects, too. How different my grandfather's life might have been had he entered into a business partnership with a worthy business partner.

Because of the One bound in swaddling clothes, we are given an opportunity to enter into a most significant partnership that brings a delightful blend of flavorings to our lives and our living. This rich spiritual aroma of our "partnership in the gospel" can permeate every part of our lives, finding its way into every affection, value, and hope that lies within us.

As this rich spiritual aroma flavors our lives, it also flavors our living. We begin to have speech "full of grace, seasoned with salt" (Colossians 4:6, NIV). We find we do "not grow weary in doing what is right" (Galatians 6:9). We find that we "can offer hospitality to one another without grumbling" (1 Peter 4:9, NIV) and that when persecuted we can "bless and do not curse" (Romans 12:14). What a rich and remarkable stew of fine flavorings and aromas our lives become when we enter into a "partnership in the gospel"!

Even from this one Advent passage, Philippians 1:3-11, we can savor the delightful taste of a life of grace found in this partnership in the gospel. However, before we explore more of the flavorings that come with a partnership in the gospel, we had better take a quick look at who is in this partnership.

When I professed my faith as a young teenager, I thought my vows were directed only toward Christ Jesus. Through the speaking of the vows, I was accepting and declaring a partnership with my Lord. I understood that I would be bound to him for the rest of my life. It was "you and me, Jesus!" However, before I finished speaking the vows, I realized that my partnership would be with more persons than just one Lord, Christ Jesus. I had joined not only Jesus but a people. You cannot join Jesus without joining the church. There would from that day forward be many others whom I would need to be faithful to, not just Jesus alone. I would, indeed, spend a lifetime serving my Lord; but I would serve him together with many service partners.

Some persons might regret being bound with so many other people, thinking that as partners are added, complications will multiply. To a degree, they are right. Having so many partners in the gospel does increase the numbers of funerals you attend, the divorces you grieve over, and the hospital visits you make to the sick, for we are to "weep with those who weep" (Romans 12:15).

Remember, however, that we are also to "rejoice with those who rejoice" (Romans 12:15). I have found that the rewards of such a broad partnership far outweigh the difficult complications. Even the occasion of weeping with a partner brings something beautiful, rich, and strong to our living. A large part of the gift that God brings to us when we are bound to Christ is the fellowship that comes with being partners in the gospel. The Christian life is a wonderful life, but it is a life that is meant to be lived with Christ and many others.

Paul had feasted on the life of grace that comes with living in partnership with Christ and his people. Paul's word in Philippians 1:3-11 is like the "ooo's" and "ahh's" that come from having tasted a remarkable specialty dish on a Christmas table. Paul discovered a growing fondness for his partners that was marked with the kind of love Christ has for all partners in the gospel. He termed this "the affection of Christ Jesus" (1:8, NIV) and it bound him with others.

In this partnership in the gospel, Paul rejoiced that he always felt the comfort and encouragement of others who were spiritually present with him, whether he was "in chains or defending and confirming the gospel" (verse 7, NIV). Furthermore, Paul was assured that he and all partners share the working of the Holy Spirit, who works untiringly to bring each partner "to completion" in love (verse 6).

Finally, with this partnership in the gospel comes the gift of prayers of petition and intercession. Paul lavished upon his partners in the gospel his well-honed prayers that they would grow in "knowledge and depth of insight" (verse 9, NIV) and be able to "discern what is best" (verse 10, NIV) and do it, living lives that were "pure and blameless" (verse 10, NIV). The result for which he longed was that those who were in this partnership in the gospel would find their lives ripe with "the fruit of righteousness" (verse 11, NIV).

How different our lives become when we enter into such a partnership with Christ and his people. The Advent and Christmas season is a time to savor the partnership we have in Christ. Let us receive the gift of partnership from the One bound in swaddling clothes.

How has your life been flavored by your partnerships?

What flavors and aromas are present with you because of your partnership in the gospel?

THE GIFT OF A CHOICE
LUKE 3:1-6

It happened during my first church appointment. I no longer remember the sermon, only the reaction afterward. Don, a parishioner, came to me and said, "You really stepped on my toes today." I understood Don to be saying that the sermon had hammered him regarding some behaviors or attitudes that needed to be changed. Somewhat surprised by his perception of my sermon, I was even more puzzled by the smile on Don's face. It looked as if Don liked having his "toes stepped on"!

I learned something about people that day while looking at Don. Something about that sermon had pushed Don into making a decision. I was seeing the afterglow on the face of one who had made a choice for God. Don had realized that there were some simple yet significant choices that needed to be made in his life, and he had made them. Don had seen how he could be a better disciple, and he had asked God to help him become a better disciple. He was

grateful for the gift of a sermon that had helped him choose.

Why would people go out into the wilderness to hear the preaching of John the Baptist? The man was notorious for stepping on toes. He was not a preacher of subtleties but a hard hitter—an in-your face kind of preacher. It had to be an uncomfortable experience to have John the Baptist gazing on you and preaching at you! Yet people went out of their way to hear this man. They went to the country in droves. Why?

Though a few may have gone out of curiosity, most went in hope of hearing a prophet put forth a powerful and challenging word from God (Matthew 11:7-9). It was a simple matter. If you went out into the wilderness to hear John the Baptist, you might come back a changed person, a true child of Abraham. However, you were not going to come out of the desert a true child of Abraham unless you made some hard choices while you were there. John the Baptist had a gift for making people choose!

Everything about John the Baptist forced people to choose. Where he lived and preached forced people to make choices. A casual trek could not get you to John the Baptist; you had to choose to go out into the wilderness country near the Jordan River to hear him preach. Even the austere wilderness seemed to surround John's sermons with a climate of choice. Life in the Judean wilderness was all business. There were few entertaining distractions. All the choices you made could affect your ability to survive. One had best to pay attention to the things that really mattered.

Who John the Baptist was forced choice as well. John the Baptist was the son of a priest. As nearly as we can tell, however, he never fulfilled any priestly duties himself, having chosen instead to live the life of a wilderness prophet. Living in the wilderness, he certainly did not look or act like a typical neighbor. His clothes were strange and his diet was bizarre (Matthew 3:4). His dress and his lifestyle showed John to be an outsider to the halls of political and religious power. His whole self-presentation suggested a judgment upon and a radical alternative to the "normal" way of life for a first-century Palestinian Jew. Thus, even a glance at John the Baptist caused persons to have to choose whether to accept his radical wisdom or reject it as too extreme.

In addition, the message of John the Baptist forced choices. His aim was to bring persons to a place where they would choose to repent. To that end, he required the repentant to mark that choice with a public act of a baptism (Luke 3:3). If you needed help seeing why you needed to repent or what you should do to live like you should, John the Baptist was eager to oblige (verses 9-14).

When John preached, he did not give you days to think over his words. There was a stated urgency in his message. In the spirit of Isaiah 40:3-5 (quoted in Luke 3:4-6), his message was that the unstoppable God was coming fast! Since God expected to find God's people holy, clean, and dedicated, John told his hearers that they had better choose now to get their lives in order by repenting and adopting new lifestyles more becoming the people of God. This was the way to prepare for God's coming. Repent! Be baptized! Choose now!

The ministry of John the Baptist resulted in persons making choices. Some, having rejected John's message, left the wilderness with faces turned downcast or angry. Many more must have worn the face of my parishioner, Don, who smiled at having been brought to a place where he could see a choice that had to be made and found himself able to make that choice, for God's sake. Those who repented and were baptized found John's message to be one of good news (verse 18).

An encounter with John the Baptist can make for a wonderful Christmas gift, but encounters with John the Baptist are rare for us these days. We do not live in an austere land but rather in a land of plenty, and the temptation is to spend too much time making insignificant choices. We are like my young son who, on his first encounter with the array of choices on the cereal aisle, stood transfixed and bedazzled. He was tortured by his inability to choose from so many cereal types.

How tragic for any of us to spend so much time making similar choices among trivial options. We harbor a desire to be presented with choices that matter. Are there choices right in front of us today that, when made, will change us to be more like Christ? Are there choices we can make that can bring us a Jesus-like ability to love or pray or laugh or know peace with God? If only someone, something, or some event could help us see what we need to choose to have a more fulfilling relationship with God and then bring us to the point of actually making that choice—now that would be a wonderful Christmas gift!

What person, experience or event has been a "John the Baptist" for you this season?

What choices is God asking you to make this Advent/Christmas season that will help you become a better disciple?

estoration

Scriptures for Advent:
The Third Sunday
Zephaniah 3:14-20
Philippians 4:4-7
Luke 3:7-18

My father had entrusted my older brother to select a Christmas present for me, his younger 7-year-old sibling. On Christmas morning, I opened the present marked "from Santa" but that was chosen by my brother and paid for by my dad. It was a plastic armored tank and tank hauling truck. I noticed that the trailer for the tank truck was not quite level, but that did not bother me much.

The condition of the new toy did bother my father, however. My dad was upset with my brother for purchasing a "second" or slightly damaged toy rather than a new unblemished one. Of course, my brother was only trying to save money; but I learned from that experience an unwritten rule that Christmas gifts should be brand new, not refurbished, old, used, or slightly damaged ones.

Adulthood has corrected my understanding of that Christmas rule, however. Some "restored" gifts become the most precious kind of Christmas presents. A once treasured heirloom, restored to its original beauty, becomes a most fantastic Christmas present. Some items, though damaged, marred, or worn out, cannot be replaced by the new. You cannot replace a damaged Stradivarius with a violin of equal worth. The sound and value of the Stradivarius can only be regained through restoration. The charm of an old mansion cannot be replaced with an expensive modern house, but that charm can return with the restoration of the grand old home.

Our covenant with God, sealed on a cross by the One bound in swaddling clothes, is a family heirloom that cannot be replaced with a new trinket. Its value lies in what this covenant makes of us, "a chosen race, a royal priesthood, a holy nation, God's own people, in order that you may proclaim the mighty acts of him who called you out of darkness into his marvelous light" (1 Peter 2:9).

Our covenant relationship with God is something that can become broken, marred, and scarred by the unfaithfulness of the people of God; but this covenant can never be replaced. If our unfaithfulness has diminished the grandness of this treasure, then what is required is a ministry of restoration. More than we want something new under the Christmas tree this year, we want to see something restored. Through the readings for the third Sunday in Advent, we will explore the restoration of beauty, gentleness, and integrity among the people of God.

THE RESTORATION OF BEAUTY
ZEPHANIAH 3:14-20

The people of the United States seem to be infatuated with beauty products. Youthful beauty appears to be admired more than the wisdom of age, and it takes a lot of work and a lot of money to hold back the marching advance of a fading beauty. We seem to be concerned about the wrong kind of ugliness and infatuated with the restoration of the wrong kind of beauty. There is a beauty that attaches to a people from a covenant relationship with a glorious God. When unfaithfulness mars that beauty and causes that beauty to fade, the people of God long for restoration.

In Deuteronomy 26:17-19, a summary of God's covenanting action is given.

Today you have obtained the LORD's agreement: to be your God; and for you to walk in his ways, to keep his statutes, his commandments, and his ordinances, and to obey him. Today the LORD has obtained your agreement: to be his treasured people, as he promised you, and to keep his commandments; *for him to set you high above all nations that he has made, in praise and in fame and in honor* [italics mine]; and for you to be a people holy to the LORD your God, as he promised.

Prophets at other times and with other words would recall this covenant with its promise.

Ezekiel spoke of how Jerusalem was like an unkempt and uncared for orphan, but God scooped the people up like a groom claiming a bride and adorned them with the trappings of blessing that made them a standout beauty among all the peoples of the earth. Bound to God in this covenant, the people had been made into a beautiful queen whose beauty was admired by the world (Ezekiel 16). Isaiah spoke in similar terms of a coming time when God would make the people of the covenant into a "crown of beauty in the hand of the LORD" (Isaiah 62:3).

Besides placing us in God's hand, God's covenant bestows on us an admirable beauty. That is as it should be. As God's treasured possession, we expect to be a beautiful people! This is not because we can make ourselves beautiful but because God, in God's redeeming work, does something extraordinary with us.

If beauty is a promise of the covenant with God, why do we people of God often consider ourselves so undesirable and unappealing? Surely we do not believe that the glamour that appeals to our culture is more beautiful than the modesty we are called to practice! That said, the beauty that God bestows on the people of the covenant can become marred, tarnished, and even taken away. When the people of God abuse the covenant that transforms what is coarse and common into the beautiful, the result is not pretty.

The prophet Zephaniah spoke to a once beautiful people who had reverted to the coarse and common. Zephaniah wrote in the last years of the 7th century B.C. during the reign of Josiah. His oracles addressed a Jerusalem poised to embark on a great undertaking for reform. King Josiah wanted to see all God's people return to faithful living under the covenant of God. Unfortunately, the reform launched by Josiah would prove too little and too late.

Zephaniah's first oracles revealed how marred Jerusalem's beauty had become. In Jerusalem, ugliness attached itself to a people who adapted their ways to those of peoples who did not know God's covenant. God's covenant was devalued; and many cried, "The LORD will not do good, / nor will he do harm" (Zephaniah 1:12).

Losing respect for God, many paid little attention to covenant obligations. As they idolized gods of power and greed, God's beautiful Zion became filled with violence and fraud (verse 9).

Having pointed out their faded beauty, Zephaniah then wrote of a coming judgment by the God of the covenant. If the people of God refused to address their ugliness, God would reveal that ugliness to the world. God's judgment (in the form of Babylonian exile) would leave them looking like the unkempt and uncared for orphans they were before they entered into covenant with God. At that time, they would no longer look like God's beautiful bride. Other nations would begin to jeer, "Is this the city that was called the perfection of beauty, / the joy of all the earth?" (Lamentations 2:15).

At last, however, Zephaniah brought God's oracle of forgiveness and hope. In this Advent reading of Zephaniah 3:14-20, we hear of a time of restoration to come after the judgment of God has done its work. The faded beauty of the people of God will be restored once the Lord takes away "the judgments against you" (verse 15).

Many people today look at the church and jeer, "Is this the city that was called the perfection of beauty, the joy of all the earth?" Although the church claims that it walks in a beautiful covenant relationship with God, others wonder why the church fails to look like God's beautiful bride. Not only is the world often disappointed with us, but also many of us in the church are saddened by our less than stellar appearance.

Like the people of Zephaniah's day, we can be loaded down with unsightly fear. Perhaps that is why God continues to say, "Do not fear, O Zion; / do not let your hands grow weak" (verse 16). Fear in a person never looks appealing. Fear hunches the shoulders, scars the soul, darts the eyes from side to side, and causes the hands to "hang limp" (verse 16, NIV). The posture of courage and confidence is much more becoming on the body.

Why is it that so many of us in church look like we are "living scared"? We are agitated by so many fears that we find it hard to take any positive action. We display a lack of confidence in "The LORD, your God, [who] is in your midst, / a warrior who gives victory" (verse 17). Some of us are living scared as we imagine being overcome by financial disasters, emotional distress, or physical decline in well-being in either ourselves or our loved ones. Still others of us are living scared as we imagine human folly bringing national, cultural, or international disasters of such magnitude that even God will be powerless to overcome them. We are a frightened people who lack faith. We need to find hope if our beauty is to be restored. "The king of Israel, the Lord, is in your midst; / you shall fear disaster no more" (verse 15).

We are also a people who need to find new strengths to help us walk as people who have a home in God's kingdom. "And I will save the lame and gather the outcast.... / At that time I will bring you home, / at the time when I gather you" (verses 19-20). No matter where we have been scattered over this earth, our home is in the great house of God. It is in that house that we learn to walk in love with our Lord. If, while living far from home, we have acquired injuries that have left us with an uncomely limp in our walk of love, we need for God to gather us back into the care of God's home. There we can have our "love gait" restored.

While we look for the restoration of our beauty this Advent/Christmas season, it would be nice to have God address our shame as well. There can be a shame that lingers when someone sees us in an "ugly" moment—when our clothes are spotted, our hair is dirty, or a blemish is at its worst.

The church has had a lot of ugly moments when it has been caught acting in ways that are embarrassing to itself and to God. The church has been caught in so many ugly moments that we sometimes wonder how even God can find in us any beauty anymore.

However, thanks be to God, our God is a God of restoration. Rather than rejecting us in our ugliness, God embraces us until we gain God's beauty again: "He will rejoice over you with gladness. / [God] will renew you in his love; / he will exult over you with loud singing / as on a day of festival" (verse 17). God will even make us "renowned and praised / among all the peoples of the earth, / when I restore your fortunes before your eyes, says the LORD" (verse 20).

With Christmas coming, we celebrate the coming of God into this world as one of us. God's incarnate love has embraced us in our ugliness. It is a good season to recall that in a covenantal embrace God has restored our beauty.

What do you see among the people of God or in yourself that are marks of a fading beauty?

What marks of beauty would you like to see restored to you this Christmas season?

THE RESTORATION OF GENTLENESS
PHILIPPIANS 4:4-7

In each church I have served, I have always sung in the choir. In all my years of singing in the choir, however, I have never intentionally sung a solo. I say "intentionally" because my wife does sometimes complain to me that I sing too loudly. Sometimes in good humor (and sometimes not), she declares that my voice stands out above other voices. I readily admit that I have heard more than one choir

director caution the bass section to be sure to "blend your voices." I also acknowledge that the comments *could* have been pointed at me.

Directors drill their choirs so that they can express to God musically a particular emotion, idea, or belief. To present a sacred piece of music well requires that the choir sometimes sing loudly and sometimes softly and sometimes at every sound level in between.

This presents something of a problem for me because I cannot sing high notes softly. Although high notes are a stretch for me, I can reach and sustain most of them if I am allowed to belt them out with full force. However, if the music requires me to sing high notes softly, then little sound comes out of my mouth at all. I have discovered that it takes a much stronger and more disciplined voice than I possess to be able to sing high notes softly.

To carry the gospel word of truth to the world, the people of God must be able to sing with more than just a loud voice. If our tone is always harsh and blaring or shrill, then our voices lack the artistic dynamics necessary to convey the "breadth and length and height and depth" of God's love (Ephesians 3:18). God must restore to God's people the ability to be gentle. "Let your gentleness be known to everyone" (Philippians 4:5).

In our society, gently spoken words are sometimes misconstrued as weak words; but gentle words often convey great power. "Through patience a ruler can be persuaded, / and a gentle tongue can break a bone" (Proverbs 25:15, NIV).

A conversation from my late 20s still demonstrates to me the power that a gentle word carries. I was talking to one of my "mothers in Christ" about Anita Bryant, the former beauty queen who had made public statements from the perspective of her faith that had been ridiculed by a harsh and biting press. I was carelessly joking about the matter and making fun of one of Anita Bryant's statements, expecting a laugh, when my spiritual mother said softly, gently, and with a pained expression on her face, four simple words: "Harsh words for Anita." I was broken . . . and silenced.

When the people of God speak with a gentle voice, they are not necessarily displaying a timid weakness. To the contrary, they are often giving evidence of an underlying power. After all, gentleness is a trait of the strong, not of the weak. Only the strong can choose to be gentle when love calls for it.

My mother taught second graders in the public schools for years and evidently made quite a mark on her students. Difficult students were regularly put into her class in the hope that, with my mother as teacher, the students' behavior might be controlled. My mother carried a reputation for having power over unruly chil-

dren, but she also had a reputation for using a soft voice. She chose to display her strength through gentleness.

When asked about her practice of speaking softly, she always said that if you spoke softly to a child, the child would not close his or her ears in great resistance.

Gentleness is a tool for communication that the people of God must pick up once again. Over time, theological pronouncements, biblical arguments, and ethical rebuttals offered only with blaring and caustic tones become indistinguishable from a "noisy gong or a clanging cymbal" (1 Corinthians 13:1) that people ignore rather than heed.

To be sure, the church has a word from God that should—and does—challenge people. From time to time, that word is likely to cause quite a stir, even among the faithful. That said, there is no good reason for the church to stir up unnecessary resistance by always using a harsh tone of voice. It would do us well to remember that "a gentle answer turns away wrath, / but a harsh word stirs up anger" (Proverbs 15:1, NIV). Every Christian should be able to be gentle when love demands it. We are told in 1 Peter 3:15-16, "Always be ready to make your defense to anyone who demands from you an accounting for the hope that is in you; yet do it with gentleness and reverence."

The ability of the people of God to be gentle when love demands it comes from the transforming work of Christ within us. Gentleness is to be a natural outgrowth of a life in Christ. Our gentleness should "be evident to all" (Philippians 4:5, NIV) because it is part of the fruit of the Spirit (Galatians 5:22-23). Gentleness comes by way of our new creation in Christ Jesus, who evidenced within himself what Paul called "meekness and gentleness" (2 Corinthians 10:1). If we, who are new creations in Christ Jesus, cannot be gentle, then there is something wrong with us that still needs to be restored to the image of Christ.

If we are not careful, gentleness can be displaced by anxiety. When we are fearful or uncertain, we often become overly tense, wary, and reactive. The slightest of insults can make us bark; a question can make us snappy in defense; a sense that we should do or say something can have us clumsily flailing away at a person or a problem. In such fear-laden moments, the self-control that gentleness requires can quickly disintegrate. Perhaps that is why gentleness and self-control are paired together in Paul's listing of spiritual fruit. In times of fear or anger, what comes to mind first is often not a gentle word. We struggle to be gentle because we do not yet have that bold confidence in God that quiets all anxiety.

A reading of Philippians 4:4-7 trumpets the assurance we have in Christ Jesus. Our fears and difficulties should not bind us, for we are a people who can "rejoice in the Lord always" (verse 4). This is so because we have seen God act powerfully on our behalf in Christ and the cross. We can afford to be gentle precisely because of our confidence that our Lord is not only strong and powerful but active and present in this world of troubles.

Furthermore, "let your gentleness be known to everyone. *The Lord is near*" (verse 5, italics mine). Our gentleness will not be inhibited by our anxieties when we have full confidence in a Lord who hears our prayers.

"Do not worry about anything, but in everything by prayer and supplication with thanksgiving let your requests be made known to God" (verse 6). We are not a people who need constantly to be "on our guard," because the kind of peace that resides in Christ has fallen on us. Paul rightly says that this "peace of God, which surpasses all understanding, will guard your hearts and your minds in Christ Jesus" (verse 7).

Songs of rejoicing, the pronouncement "the Lord is near," expectant prayers, and the peace of Christ—it is beginning to sound a lot like Christmas. Today is an excellent time to ask God to restore our gentleness.

How capable of gentleness are you at this time in your life?

What is love demanding from you: a gentle word or a gentle touch?

THE RESTORATION
OF INTEGRITY
LUKE 3:7-18

Nobody enjoys having her or his integrity questioned. Challenge me on something I have done or criticize me for a mistake I have made, and I can live with that (with some discomfort, to be sure). Challenge me on my integrity or point your criticism at "who I am," however, and you are likely to receive a fight-to-the death defense from me. To question my integrity is to declare to me that I am not who I think I am! My instinct for self-preservation kicks in, warning me that my personal integrity is under attack and that my "self" is at risk. A successful blow might leave my self-understanding of "who I am" broken to pieces.

Nobody wants to go through that kind of emotional devastation. Yet an encounter with an agent of God's truth can challenge our integrity and leave our self-image in pieces; but where there is a godly challenge to our integrity, there is also the possibility of restoration. John the Baptist was an agent of God's truth. Christ Jesus is a minister of restoration, restoring a holy integrity to the disciple of Christ.

The task given John the Baptist is more involved than that of simply announcing the coming of the Lord. A slightly better description of the task of John the Baptist would be that he was to serve as a "warm-up" band to the coming star attraction. I have been to a few rock concerts in my day and have experienced the role of the warm-up band. The warm-up band is clearly second to the star attraction; and its task is to play the music that will adjust the attitude of the audience, putting the audience in the right frame of mind to receive with enthusiasm the main band.

In a similar vein, John the Baptist was to preach the message that would adjust the attitude of those who came to the wilderness by pointing them toward the coming Jesus. Only so would they be ready to receive the ministry of the Lord. John the Baptist did his task well. His edgy presentation was not exactly something one "enjoyed"; but when the presentation was over, many found themselves in the right attitude to embrace the ministry of the coming Lord Jesus.

John the Baptist was a master at creating an attitude of dissatisfaction among his listeners. Listening to John's preaching spurred dissatisfaction with one's own integrity—a harmonious union of who one claims to be in God and who one actually is.

Based on the example of his preaching style in Luke 3:7-18, John began his sermons with an opening barrage on the integrity of the listeners, shocking them with the possibility that they may not be who they think themselves to be. John said, "You brood of vipers!" (verse 7). Few of us think of ourselves as people with the character of a snake. John's first word is to question not one's actions but one's presumption to be a true child of Abraham (verses 7-8).

Presumption is often a hardened defense against true integrity. When I presume that I am a trustworthy, dedicated, and faithful lover of my Lord Jesus, my presumption can protect me from an uncomfortable and revealing inspection of my true self before God.

My own salvation story reveals such a battle with presumption. I grew up in a fine Christian family and was raised in a fine church. I had encounters with God that were true and challenging; yet somehow I entered my college years with my well-defended presumptions about myself intact. I was convinced that, in spite of any evidence to the contrary, I was a better-than-most disciple with no unsightly areas of gross sin that offered any real offense to my Lord. Thus I was "okay" with God, and certainly God was "okay" with me.

I carried this presumption through college, seminary, and my first years of serving a church as a United Methodist pastor. It was not until I turned 30 that I ran into a John the Baptist (a community of Christians that served me as an agent of God's truth) who questioned my presumption. The process I went through could be compared to an encounter with John the Baptist. I was never assaulted with name-calling accusations; but in this community of Christians, my presumption was assaulted by the holy, loving, and dedicated quality of the Christians I was partnered with in community.

As I watched their lives of humble, joyful, sacrificial love, my own life in the Lord was called into question. These people had fruit in their lives that looked like what one should expect to see in a true child of God. The integrity evidenced in those who could humbly claim to be Christian and at the same time live Christ-like lives helped me become dissatisfied with my integrity. I grew weary of putting on a show and of living lies. I yearned to have some integrity restored to my life with the Lord.

John the Baptist was a master at creating an attitude of dissatisfaction in his listeners. Having softened the defenses of his listeners by an opening barrage on their presumptions of integrity, all John had to do was point out the incongruities between who they claimed to be (true children of Abraham) and how they lived their lives. Each listener had different incongruities, but the result was a dissatisfaction that had the listener wanting a remedy.

The remedy John proposed was twofold. The first step was to go through a "baptism of repentance" (verse 3). The repentance demanded was not an easy one. The penitent was to reveal his or her new perceptions through a public confession. To be baptized was to admit publicly that your previous claims to be a true son or daughter of Abraham had been bogus and that you needed to be born again as a true (faithful) son or daughter of the Lord. However, the second step of the remedy was not found in the ministry of John the Baptist but in the ministry of Jesus.

John can bring dissatisfaction with integrity, but only Christ Jesus can bring the restoration of integrity. John pointed to a Lord who would baptize "with the Holy Spirit and fire" (verse 16). The prophet Ezekiel had foretold a time when a water of baptism would "cleanse you from all your impurities" and a "new heart" would be given and a "new spirit" put into God's people. The result would be that the people of God would actu-ally be able to keep the ways of the Lord (Ezekiel 36:25-27).

Jesus, coming with a baptism of fire and the Holy Spirit, fulfilled this prophecy. The fire was the purifying action of Christ on the repentant. Christ burns away that which has us living deceitful lives. The Holy Spirit speaks of the age-old promise to forge a new heart within us that can house the Spirit of God. The result of this ministry of restoration is that the people of God are able to live as the followers of Christ they claim to be!

Where, in this Advent/ Christmas season, are you running into a "John the Baptist" who is making you dissatisfied with your life in God?

What makes your hopes for restored integrity realistic?

Peace

Scriptures for Advent:
The Fourth Sunday
Micah 5:2-5a
Hebrews 10:5-10
Luke 1:39-45

The season of Advent/Christmas carries its familiar sounds. In the coming weeks, we expect to hear hopeful sighs, squeals of surprise, happy greetings, and joyful voices.

Of course, the Advent/Christmas season also brings sounds we would rather not hear. The grief experienced by spending a Christmas without a loved one can cause the sound of weeping. Disappointment in the face of soaring expectations of life can bring the voice of irritation. Pressure and crowds can bring the harsh tones of ugly expletives. Sometimes the presence of our relatives come home for Christmas brings as many sounds of conflict as it does sounds of laughter.

The Advent/Christmas season creates a lot of different sounds, not all of which are soothing, warm, and joyous. Scripture speaks of Herod's rejection of the infant King; and the result is the sound of "wailing and loud lamentation, / Rachel weeping for her children" (Matthew 2:18). These are the sounds of war, not peace; and they are spurred by the coming of the One bound in swaddling clothes.

Into this harsh world that finds people at conflict with God, with each other, and within themselves, the Prince of Peace makes his entrance to claim his territory. We can hardly expect the coming of the One bound in swaddling clothes to always be accompanied with the calming tune of "Silent Night." Yet it is right for us to expect to hear the sound of peace at Christmas. We should be able to hear "Silent Night" among all the other sounds that this season brings, for "he is our peace" (Ephesians 2:14) and has come into this world proclaiming peace.

Through these Scriptures of the fourth Sunday in Advent, we will look to the peace that comes with the One bound in swaddling clothes. Through Micah 5:2-5a, we will meditate on the peace that is coming with a righteous king. With Hebrews 10:5-10, we will look at a peace that is accessible to us through sacrifice. With the Gospel passage of Luke 1:39-45, we will explore the peace that can only come with our acceptance of God's mission.

PEACE THROUGH
A RIGHTEOUS KING
MICAH 5:2-5a

We in the United States are not unfamiliar with promises of peace and prosperity; we hear them every election year: "If I am elected, I will. . . ." The words flow from the candidate that would have us believe the difference between peace and war or calamity and prosperity lie with our choice for president. This is not to say that leadership makes no difference on the future of a nation. By and large, however, our experience is that presidents have a much smaller role in bringing a promised peace and prosperity than their election speeches would claim.

As a result, many of us become a little jaundiced about election promises. While we would prefer to hear a candidate speak of a coming peace and prosperity rather than a promise of chaos and dire poverty, few of us actually think candidates for office come with guarantees of promised results. We have seen promises come and leaders go. Too often we

end up disappointed when we compare what was pledged to what was produced. We can be left wondering, *Is there really a leader for our people who could make a difference?* The prophecy of Micah: 5:2-5a claims that a leader is coming who will make all the difference!

As much as we in our time might carry doubts about what a leader can do, the people of the time of Micah's prophecy would likely carry even more suspicion than us. The northern kingdom of Israel and the southern kingdom of Judah had experienced king after king who could not usher in a time of secure prosperity.

Scholars disagree as to whether Micah 5:2-5a was directed toward people living with the threat of Assyrian domination (the northern kingdom of Israel fell to Assyria in 722 B.C.) or aimed toward a later people who were in exile after the southern kingdom of Judah fell to Babylonia in 586 B.C. In either instance, a realistic appraisal of chances for peace and prosperity did not include much hope.

The people of God living on this little piece of land in the Middle East seemed always to be surrounded by one bully nation after another. Each war brought devastation. Some other nations might make an economy from the occupations of conquering and pillaging, but the people of God could not make a living from it nor would their God allow them to try.

In the land of the promise and among the people of the covenant, without peace there was no prosperity. Yet peace seemed always to be at risk. Threats to peace could always be detected just over the time horizon, and the kings of the people of God had neither the people count nor the military clout to seize the future and force a secure peace by strength of arms.

To a people who had such dim prospects for peace came the prophetic Word of the Lord found in the Book of Micah. The word Micah brought spoke of a ruler who would usher in a long-yearned for peace. In spite of their past experience with kings, this leader would make all the difference! This ruler would be different from other kings they had had. This leader would bring a different result through his reign.

In either our time or the time of Micah, would we be naïve to believe that any leader, no matter how unique compared to our past experiences, could bring such peace into this world? There is no doubt that the truth-claim spoken by Micah the prophet was a fantastic one.

The prophesied differences between this designated ruler and past kings of Israel and Judah were fantastic and so were his origins. Unlike rulers who rise to the throne due to claims of genetic lineage or schemes rooted in their ambition, the origin of this one's rise to the seat of power would lie in the ancient purposes of God. God would bring forth this ruler out of God's own ancient promise.

This ruler was one "whose origin is from of old, / from ancient days" (Micah 5:2). This ruler would not rise to power out of his own self-determination, but out of God's loving intention for the world.

The ends toward which this ruler would bend his power were equally fantastic. "From you shall come forth *for me* [italics mine] one who is to rule in Israel" (verse 2). This ruler would rule according to God's purpose, not contrary to God's purpose. This ruler would seek to serve God's pleasure, not his own.

This ruler would also be fantastic in that, unlike so many rulers of Israel and Judah, he would "stand" (verse 4) in the Lord. Other kings had regularly fallen to temptations of idolatry and injustice; this ruler would be able to hold to righteousness.

Finally, this ruler would "feed his flock in the strength of the LORD, / in the majesty of the name of the LORD his God" (verse 4). By relying on God's strength rather than his own, this ruler would raise a people who lived by the strength of God rather than relied on their own strength. These people would become a people of such confidence and trust in God that they would be able to accomplish much while fearing little, for they would know their Lord was with them.

The result of the reign of this different ruler would also be fantastic. "And they shall live secure, for now he shall be great / to the ends of the earth; / and he shall be the one of peace" (verses 4-5). Rather than the usual disappointment that follows a king's promise of peace and prosperity, the reputation of this ruler would actually win a worldwide following, helping all to find security under his powerful reign of peace.

Can we believe such a prophecy? Some, of course, do not believe. Others do believe but still await the arrival of the prophesied ruler. However, those of us who celebrate the birth of the One bound in swaddling clothes see in Jesus the ruler promised in Micah 5:2-5a.

We find his origin in the covenant promises of old that speak of One coming from Bethlehem. We understand Jesus as one who served God's ends in all things. We see Jesus as one who was able to stand in righteousness. We believe that through Jesus, Christians find God's strength and power to live a holy life, a life dedicated to the purposes of God.

We who celebrate the birth of the One bound in swaddling clothes have come to believe this fantastic prophecy of a different kind of ruler. We have seen that portion of the prophecy fulfilled in Christ Jesus; but what about the fantastic result that is to come from this ruler's reign? Where is the security and peace that was to be established and would extend to the ends of the earth? We do not know that kind of fantastic peace and neither does the world—not yet at any rate.

Some might take a quick look at our strife-laden world and use what they see as evidence to discredit the prophecy of Micah 5:2-5a and the supposedly naïve persons who would be so gullible as to believe such a prophecy. However, we who know Christ Jesus need not be discouraged by such criticism. For us, the fulfillment of the first portion of Micah's fantastic prophecy merely increases our certainty that the rest of the prophecy will come to pass.

We have seen and do bear witness to a fantastic ruler; and there will come a time when the reign of this ruler will be fully established, and the world will witness a fantastic peace. The different ruler, the One bound in swaddling clothes, will make all the difference!

How does believing Christ Jesus to be the ruler promised in Micah 5:2-5a affect your hope for peace in the world?

How does having "the one of peace" (Micah 5:5) as your ruler change how you live and witness for world peace?

PEACE THROUGH SACRIFICE
HEBREWS 10:5-10

I do not want to call it what it has traditionally been called: a sin offering. Even though Scripture itself calls it a "sin" offering, I prefer to think of it as a "peace" offering. What is the offering for?

When I utter words I should not have said, I must find a way to bridge the gap between us if our relationship is to be mended. If I want us to be at peace again, I must consider presenting a thoughtful gift to launch the recovery process. The gift in question is a "peace offering."

A peace offering is something that is seen, touched, and appreciateed, a concrete symbol of my apology and hope for our future. This gift must also be a sacrificial gift that "costs me something."

A peace offering must not only represent me but also demonstrate that I have put something of myself into this gift that I extend into the gap between us. This sacrificial peace offering must also be able to speak some words for me. It must say, "I was wrong. I am sorry. I value what we have together. I want to have peace again, so we can enjoy our life together."

Would flowers make a good peace offering? Or is the offense bad enough to warrant a piece of jewelry? Should I say it with diamonds?

"Sacrifices and offerings you have not desired, ... / in burnt offerings and sin offerings / you have taken no pleasure" (Hebrews verses 5-6). Can we bring flowers to the Almighty and expect reconciliation? Can we give diamonds to our God and expect peace?

Even in the world of human relationships, our peace offerings do not always bridge the gaps of estrangement. Sometimes our offenses against other human beings are just too great for flowers or even diamonds to reach across the distance between us. Sometimes our offenses have simply been too constant and too many. In this case, if words of apology are to be forthcoming and sincere or if any hope for peace is to be re-established, it will not come from our efforts for peace; it will have to come by way of the unmerited grace and forgiveness of the one whom we have offended.

Our peace offerings of flowers or diamonds cannot bridge the gap created by our offenses against the God who loves us. The offenses have been too big and too many. God, with unmerited grace and forgiveness, must take the first step into the alienating chasm that exists between God and us.

God, in fact, has already taken that step by entering this world as the One bound in swaddling clothes. In Jesus, God offered his own body as a sin offering on the cross. It is not the sacrificial gifts we bring to God that will reestablish peace, no matter if our peace offerings are small or large, cheap or expensive, costing us nothing or costing us everything. God must take the first step, and God has done this! God has taken this crucial step through the sacrifice of Christ Jesus (Colossians 1:19-20).

Much of the Book of Hebrews, and verses 5-10a, was written to help us gauge the true worth of Jesus' sacrifice on the cross. Most of us could use some help in that endeavor. I was not raised in a culture that understood priestly law or was accustomed to the practice of religious sacrifice. As a result, I am deficient in understanding one of the love languages of God: the language of sacrifice.

"God's love was revealed among us in this way: God sent his only Son into the world so that we might live though him. In this is love, not that we loved God but that he loved us and sent his Son to be the atoning sacrifice for our sins" (1 John 4:9-10). The language of the Temple sacrifice speaks of the enduring love of a Holy God who bears with an unholy people.

Has it occurred to you what great trouble our unholy presence has created for the Holy One who loves us? To be sure, in our short-sighted assessment of ourselves in which we tend to gloss over our shortcomings, we have difficulty grasping how our presence could ever be intolerably offensive to God. Yet the language of Temple sacrifice teaches us that, due to our sin, we cannot even approach the presence of God without giving offense.

Because of our sin, we require a priest who has been washed clean through a meticulous ceremony of cleansing. Only a priest who is truly clean can approach the altar

on our behalf (Hebrews 9). There the priest will make our sin offering before God. There, an unblemished animal, blemished now by our sin, will be slain in our stead to show the severity of our transgression before God.

When the Holy and the unholy come into contact, the death of the unholy is the result. Our sin is expensive; it costs a life. However, if the language of sacrifice speaks blaringly of our offense to God's holiness, it speaks even more loudly of God's grace.

God's love for us is so great and God's desire to dwell with us is so deep that God lovingly made a way of reconciliation and forgiveness available to us. By means of this way, God and God's beloved people can continue to live together.

At first, the way God provided was cleansing through repeated Temple sacrifices of animals by ceremonially consecrated priests. Now, says the writer of Hebrews, God has made available an eternal way of reconciliation and forgiveness that makes it possible for God and his people to dwell together forever. God has offered himself as the sacrificial animal and the consecrated priest.

"Sacrifices and offerings you have not desired, / but a body you have prepared for me" (10:5). The body of the One once bound in swaddling clothes allows God to be the unblemished lamb of sacrifice offered in our stead as a sin offering (1 Corinthians 15:3). It allows God to serve as the consecrated priest who approaches the very throne of God on our behalf. In short, it is God's great sacrifice that brings lasting peace, not our little peace offerings.

At every turn, I find myself more and more in debt to God. God, out of love for me, made the sacrificial offering that should have been mine to make. I was the one who did the injury to our relationship, but God accomplished the reconciliation. I was the one who caused the gaping wound of estrangement, but God stepped into the gap to establish peace. It was my sin that made me an offense to God's holiness; but through the loving sacrifice of Christ Jesus, I was washed clean of my sin in forgiveness.

The God I have been invited to walk with will always "out-love" me, and for that I am grateful. The best I can do in response is offer my own body as a "living sacrifice" (Romans 12:1) in response to the sacrifice Christ made for me. My sacrifice is to "live in love, as Christ loved us and gave himself up for us, a fragrant offering and sacrifice to God" (Ephesians 5:2). The perspective of Hebrews helps me gauge the true worth of Christ Jesus' sacrifice on the cross. The love I encounter in that sacrifice is truly worthy of my life.

What kinds of offerings have you made to try to find peace with God?

What one word would most accurately describe your response to the peace God has offered you?

Where is God calling you this Advent/Christmas season to "live in love as Christ loved us"?

PEACE THROUGH ACCEPTANCE
LUKE 1:39-45

"Blessed is she who has believed that what the Lord has said to her will be accomplished!" (Luke 1:45, NIV).

One of my favorite television shows is the adventure series *Mission: Impossible.* The opening scene always entailed a mysterious voice proposing a preposterous mission to a daring crew of special agents. The mission was so dangerous that no one (not even the government) could in good conscience force the agents to accept the undertaking. So somewhere in the proposal the words would eventually be spoken: "Your mission, *should you decide to accept it . . .*" Throughout the long history of the show, I do not believe one agent ever once said, "No, I'm sorry; I can't accept that mission. I just don't believe I'm the person to accomplish that mission."

"Your mission, *should you decide to accept it . . .*" One day (nothing in the story suggests it was a night visit), Mary received a troubling visit from a mysterious messenger proposing a seemingly preposterous mission.

According to the angel Gabriel, the plan was for Mary, though unmarried and a virgin, to give birth to a son through the power of the Holy Spirit. She was to name the boy Jesus. The boy would become great and even come to be called the Son of God, reigning over a kingdom that would never end (Luke 1:26-38).

Such a mission easily outdistances any that the television scriptwriters for *Mission: Impossible* ever produced, for the stakes of this mission were incomparably higher. In his book *Peculiar Treasures,* Frederick Buechner catches the tension of this moment well:

> He [Gabriel] told her what the child was to be named, and who he was to be, and something about the mystery that was to come upon her. "You mustn't be afraid, Mary," he said.
>
> As he said it, he only hoped she wouldn't notice that beneath the great, golden wings he himself was trembling with fear to think that the whole future of creation hung now on the answer of a girl.[1]

It does not surprise me to find Mary distressed by the impossible mission proposed by this improbable messenger. I have certainly become quite distressed over matters far less important. I seem to be one of those persons who has a low tolerance for tension. I enjoy my peace tremendously. My peace is as important to me as my old worn-out reclining chair is comfortable, and I want to stay in it. When my peace is disturbed by an unwanted intrusion, I want to see the disturbance quelled in short

order so that I can get my peace back quickly.

With this visit from Gabriel, Mary has had something quite disturbing inserted into her peaceful state of affairs. She is distressed, and I do not envy her—but I should learn from her! Mary's path to peace is to believe and accept the mission God gave her. From Mary, I have learned that when a messenger from the Lord shows up in your room and asks you to do something for God, you will not find peace until you answer yes!

All of us who have been Christians for a while have probably received a few messengers with impossible mission proposals. Impossible missions are part and parcel of what comes with the call to follow Christ Jesus. We are asked to become fishers of people (Mark 1:16) and to "cure the sick, raise the dead, cleanse the lepers, cast out demons" (Matthew 10:8). We are asked to "proclaim the good news to the whole creation" (Mark 16:15) and to feed the hungry, clothe the naked, take care of the sick, visit those in prison, and welcome the stranger (Matthew 25:31-46).

The mysterious messenger may come to us through Scripture that is read, through a word that is spoken, through a dream, a vision, or a passion that will not be quiet and will not let us go. The impossible mission put forth may be lacking in detail; or it may come with details of name, place, and specific task. Either way, the Lord has a saving habit of showing up in what we think is the privacy of our lives. Again and again, God intrudes into our peace with a proposal to join our Lord in an impossible mission. When this visitation happens to us, the only way to find peace is to go along with Christ. Accept the mission!

One of the first barriers we encounter when we are asked to accept God's mission for our lives is the barrier of our own unbelief. We may have significant doubt that the mysterious messenger is truly from God.

Before Mary could say yes to God's mission assignment, she had to be convinced that the angel who was saying such things to her was from God, not that trickster, Satan. "Blessed is she who has believed what *the Lord* has said to her" (Luke 1:45, NIV; emphasis mine). Mary had to believe that the mission proposal really was from God.

Many of us struggle at that same point of belief. The world is filled with messengers who regularly invite us to join missions that are counter to God's purpose. We could mistakenly say yes to a mission that arises from our unholy passions of pride, anger, or fear rather than holy passions grounded in our desire for the kingdom of God. However, while we must discern whether the call we are receiving is in line with the purposes of God's kingdom, we must never be so suspicious that

we reject God's messengers out of hand. Quite frankly, we ought to be expecting God to issue invitations for mission, not assuming that God will never call.

The more likely danger that you and I will encounter is not the danger of accepting a false mission but the danger of rejecting one mission call after another because we do not believe God would ask us to do something. Throughout history, Christians have experienced Christ invite even the least and the last of all persons to join with God on impossible missions. In fact, even the simple act of saying yes to God requires us to join God's mission!

Mary crossed the first barrier of unbelief (that the messenger may not be of God) and then encountered another barrier of unbelief. Mary had to believe that "what the Lord has said to her *will be accomplished*" (Luke 1:45 NIV; emphasis mine). Before Mary could accept the impossible mission from God, she had to believe that, in God, the mission was not impossible at all. Rather, it could be accomplished! God would supply her with what she needed for her part in the mission. By saying yes she was not binding herself to a lost cause that would create eternal frustration but rather to God's final victory of peace.

You need to know that nothing causes more frustration in me than to be given an assignment that I cannot hope to complete. The expectations I place on myself for accomplishment, combined with the possibility of failure because of my inadequacy, make a concoction that throws me in a tizzy.

How odd, then, that God called me to become the pastor of a church! I have accepted and taken my place in a mission that is much bigger than my ability, my enthusiasm, and the time that I have been allotted. In the service of my Lord, I regularly encounter confusion and hardship, some suffering, and occasional persecution. Yet I find peace, not continual frustration, in this calling. That verifies for me the truth of 2 Corinthians 12:9, "My grace is sufficient for you, for power is made perfect in weakness."

All of us who say yes to God's mission will, like Mary, find ourselves in over our heads. Our abilities and our love will fall far short of what is needed. We can be grateful, however, that God's grace will be more than sufficient. Time and again, we will be humbled by the fact that God manages to get something accomplished through us.

Truly blessed are we when we believe that what the Lord has said will be accomplished!

In what ways do you find yourself in over your head in relation to God's call on your life?

How are you finding God's grace sufficient for you to accomplish your heavenly assignments?

---

[1] From *Peculiar Treasures: A Biblical Who's Who,* by Frederick Buechner (Harper & Row Publishers, 1979); page 39.

Savior

Scriptures for Christmas Eve:
Isaiah 9:2-7
Titus 2:11-14
Luke 2:1-20

With the words "I can do it myself," my four-year-old nephew grabbed the plate of spaghetti and began to totter across the great expanse of carpet that lay between the kitchen and the dining room table. I appreciated my nephew's "can-do" attitude, but I also quickly considered the bad attitude that I might encounter if the parsonage committee learned of a newly acquired giant red stain on the parsonage carpet.

I knew from personal experience that the spaghetti was slippery and hard to keep on the plate. I quickly calculated the odds and determined that all the can-do spirit in the world would not have my nephew successful in crossing the terrain to the table with the spaghetti still on his plate.

My nephew saw himself as capable and needing no help, but his judgment did not line up with reality. I decided to intervene and save myself a meeting with the parsonage committee.

Certainly a can-do attitude can take us far in life, but a can-do attitude cannot take us as far in life as we need to go. To live the life of love that God sets before us is a task too large to tackle with a can-do attitude alone. We are not able to "do it myself." We need help and lots of it. We need a saving God.

It is said that when a turtle is seen perched on top of a fence post, one thing that you can be certain of is that the turtle had help getting there. The person of faith knows that he or she is that turtle on the fence post. Whatever progress we have made in living a life of love, it is because we have been helped to get there by a God who is eager to save.

Through each Scripture reading assigned for Christmas Eve, we will consider afresh this God who is so eager to save that he was willing to come into this world bound in swaddling clothes. With the reading from Isaiah we will contemplate a powerful Savior. In the Titus passage, we will gaze at a redeeming Savior. With the passage from Luke, we will look upon an inviting Savior.

A POWERFUL SAVIOR
ISAIAH 9:2-7

This passage from Isaiah 9:2-7 reads like a casserole of biblical literary forms. It is mostly a praise hymn, with a dash of coronation ceremony and a dollop of hopeful prophecy dropped in the mix. The combination makes for a satisfying meal for those who, having lived under oppression, are now hungry for the power of God to act on their behalf.

If *power* can be defined as "the ability to enact change," it is little wonder that people want power. Possessing enough power can assure the powerful that no unwelcome circumstances or conditions have to be endured for long. Changes can be made!

Life is experienced quite differently by those who have little power. Those who lack power have little hope of changing the negative circumstances and conditions that work against them. If the powerless are to find relief from harsh realities, they must either locate hidden power of their own or—more commonly—wait for the powerful to act on their behalf.

The powerless people of Judah had seen little progress on either count. On the world stage, Judah would certainly have been numbered among the powerless. Her meager military strength would never be able to stand up for long to the military might of the powerful nations she encountered, one after another, in a series of repeated threats and invasions.

Furthermore, within Judah's own political arena, a privileged class held tightly to economic and political power and often used that power to its own benefit. Prophets had long pointed out the terrible injustices that ran rampant in the little kingdom. They repeatedly railed against those who used positions of power and privilege to take advantage of those among God's people who had little economic or political power.

If the only hope that the powerless in Judah had for seeing life improve lay with the privileged using their power on behalf of the powerless, then there was very little hope indeed. Then, as now, the powerful of the world rarely had either the time or the energy to share with the downtrodden! Oppressed and beaten down by the world, the weak and the poor of Judah could not see any source of great power willing to counter the harsh realities and change life for the better. The powerless had to turn their gaze beyond the landscape of the world to the one who had initially brought them up out of the land of Egypt to locate a great power willing to act on their behalf.

Power, in and of itself, is not a bad thing. One's power (the ability to enact change) can be derived from one's wealth, position, reputation, personality, knowledge, wisdom, accomplishments, ability to persuade, talent, and a host of other sources.

It is certainly possible that whatever power you and I have accumulated was gained justly. More important than how we gain our power, however, is how we use our power. Do we use it to serve ourselves? If so, our power is rendered unjust in the eyes of God.

Like a factory, the world seems to produce one powerful person after another who uses his or her power to benefit further the powerful. Only God, not the world, is able to produce a people who are willing to use their power on behalf of the powerless. Verses 2-7 look forward to the time when God produces this remarkable person of power.

In this passage, we hear the exuberant praise of a powerless people who, at long last, have witnessed a great power working for them, not against them. That great power is almighty God who has intervened on their behalf. Their powerful God has enacted changes so sweeping in effect that it is as if night has now become day (verse 2). The borders of the nation, once hard pressed, have now been expanded (verse 3). The foreign military threat has been neutralized (verses 4-5). Wealth is returning to the people.

Giddy with what has been witnessed, the people—filled with new hope—now envision the next powerful change to be enacted by their almighty God. Now God will work within the nation itself and enact the changes needed to bring a better life. God has placed among them a powerful ruler. This powerful One is now only a child (verse 6); but unlike other kings the world produces, this King will use his power on behalf of the powerless. This King will bring peace, justice, and righteousness (verse 7).

Has the world yet seen this remarkable person whom the powerless longed for? Some biblical scholars attribute the coronation aspect of verses 2-7 to King Hezekiah, but the referent cannot be certain.

It is quite possible that the original intent was to point to Hezekiah, for Hezekiah was one of the few kings of Judah who attempted to use his power on behalf of God and the powerless who dwell in God's heart. Yet if this passage really did refer to Hezekiah, it is hard to avoid thinking that the passage greatly exaggerated the impact of his birth.

The one referred to as "Wonderful Counselor, Mighty God, Everlasting Father, Prince of Peace," whose accomplishments will include "endless peace" and a rule upheld "with justice and with righteousness from this time onward and forevermore" seems to speak of a personage and accomplishments far greater in scope than that of any known king of the people of God. The one exception is the One who was born in Bethlehem, bound in swaddling clothes, and found lying in a manger. Christians can look to this peculiarly prophetic passage, consider Jesus, and become mesmerized by the remarkable love of God.

From time to time, we read in the newspaper of a hospital nursery where a baby's name has been wrongly applied to another infant. The results of such a wrongful appellation are tragic.

At first, applying such powerful names as "Wonderful Counselor, Mighty God, Everlasting Father, Prince of Peace" to a baby bound in swaddling clothes and found lying in a manger seems to be tragic folly. The contrast between the names and the child are too great, for the names given the child are names that should only be rightfully applied to God.

Yet in that peculiarity resides the truth that confronts us so profoundly. When we gaze at Jesus, we do see the God of power whose love is so remarkable that he chose to slip into our world as a child, dwell among us who are powerless, and use his saving power on our behalf. The people of God who lived in the time of Isaiah gave witness to a miracle: They saw someone of great power (almighty God) using that power on behalf of the powerless. We give witness to the same kind of miracle in the birth,

life, death, resurrection, and return of this One who was once bound in swaddling clothes. The God of power is a powerful Savior.

The Scripture passage concludes with an explanation for the miracles that have been reported and those that are projected: "The zeal of the LORD of hosts will do this" (verse 7). Many religions describe the god they worship as a God of great power. However, few go on to say that their God of power is zealous to use that divine power on behalf of those who have no power of their own.

In God's zeal, we discover something astounding about the nature of God's love. The love of our powerful God is so great he willingly laid down his life of power for us (John 15:13). If we find ourselves mesmerized by the remarkable love we see in this One once bound in swaddling clothes, we need to let that same love do its mighty work in us. As it does, we will find ourselves compelled (2 Corinthians 5:14, NIV) to "lay down our lives for one another" (1 John 3:16). The best way to serve our Lord, our powerful Savior, is by using our power on behalf of others.

In what ways are you present with and available to the powerful?

In what ways are you present with and available to the powerless?

How are you using the power you have been given on behalf of the powerless?

A REDEEMING SAVIOR
TITUS 2:11-14

It is certain that the One bound in swaddling clothes came into this world to be a redeeming Savior. What is not certain is whether you and I truly see how dire our need is for such a redeeming Savior. If we naively think that we can master the art of living with just a good example (left to us as a courtesy by Jesus) or a life lesson or two taught by our Lord, we are sadly mistaken. Persons who acknowledge that they could use a little help but have no real need of God's redemption have either led a charmed life or never had to plumb the depths of who they are.

If all we need in this life is "a little help," than surely Christ Jesus paid an absurdly heavy price to send us a little aide. However, Scripture says Christ Jesus "gave himself for us that he might redeem us from all iniquity and purify for himself a people of his own" (verse 14). The price paid staggers the imagination, but nothing less could have redeemed us.

The language of redemption was meant to be a weighty one that carried a punch. Unfortunately, the language of redemption has lost much of its power in this modern world where the usual referent for *redemption* is trading stamps or coupons.

In the biblical world, however, the language of redemption was used to address the matter of emancipation for slaves or rescue of those condemned to death. When the words *redeem* and *redemption* refer to matters of that gravity, they possess their rightful impact. Our need for redemption is a grave matter. Our indebtedness to a redeeming Savior is colossal.

Titus was "left . . . behind" (1:5) to give oversight to the Christian church (or churches) on the island of Crete. As time passed, however, Titus realized that he also needed advice if he were to accomplish the task set before him.

The problem for Titus was the Cretan populace he had been charged to "put in order" (1:5). People of the island of Crete had a reputation that evidenced the need for their redemption. "It was one of them, their very own prophet, who said, / 'Cretans are always liars, vicious brutes, lazy gluttons'" (1:12). Among the Greeks, to *Cretize* meant "to lie and deceive."[1] Furthermore, an old Greek proverb stated that of all the peoples whose name began with *C*, the three worst were the Cretans, the Cappadocians, and the Cilicians.[2]

While we must not give too much credence to the prejudiced opinion of the Greek writer who supposed that the people raised on the island of Crete were markedly worse in character than other people, we can still sympathize with Titus and the Christian churches. On the island of Crete, to bring a person into godly living required that the person be set free or be redeemed from the ungodly ways of living found among the Cretans.

We have, of course, the same difficult task to accomplish in our churches today. There is an ungodly way of living that stakes its claim on the people of this land. The "American way of life" must not be equated with the "godly way of life." If we have come to think and act more like the people around us than we think and act like Jesus, we have a real problem. Our call is to "live lives that are self-controlled, upright, and godly" (2:12). Is that the kind of living that we see around us? We, like Titus, are surrounded by Cretans; in fact, we, too, may be Cretans. If we are to become godly, we must be set free from the cultural character traits that hold us in bondage. We need redemption.

Paul (or the Pauline writer of Titus) reminded Titus and the people of the churches on Crete that they, like those around them, were "slaves to various passions and pleasures" (3:3).

We do not control our passions; our passions control us. Our passions flavor our thoughts and spike our actions. Our passions can move us toward godly living or propel us toward wickedness.

It is the ungodly passions that destroy us. Ungodly passions are like weeds that take over the lawn, turning everything ugly. New hates, new lusts, new resentments, new fears, and new prejudices keep springing up like weeds where they are not wanted. The weeds spring up in every aspect of our living and destroy a marriage here, a close friendship there, perhaps even a job. Over time they can spread throughout an entire populace and destroy a society.

We come into this world bearing the seeds of ungodly passions in our lives. Some of those seeds sink roots and grow while we are being cultivated in our family of origin. Other weeds take their first footing from exposure to the neighbor's yard, so to speak. Some ungodly passions spread to us from the culture that is around us. Once we are overrun with ungodly passions, however, we cannot live the godly lives Christ Jesus intended for us. We just cannot seem to get rid of the weeds.

Like you, I know what it is to have weeds in my lawn that I cannot get rid of. Renouncing our inclinations toward worldliness is never as easy as just saying no. There always seem to be more worldly inclinations than we can successfully fight; and when we think we have a worldly passion conquered, it has a resilient way of coming back to life.

To have the ability to say no to worldly passions, we will need a lot of help from One who is not overrun with them. Successful training to "renounce impiety and worldly passions" can only come after "the grace of God has appeared, bringing salvation to all" (verses 11-12). The grace of God that has appeared, which brings to us salvation, is our Lord Jesus Christ, the redeeming Savior, the One bound in swaddling clothes.

A redeeming Savior is needed to free us of worldly passions and plant in us the passions of Christ Jesus. We need to undergo "passion-replacement" therapy where the passions that energize us toward iniquity are purified from us and new passions that energize us toward "good deeds" (verse 14) are planted, making us "eager to do what is good" (verse 14, NIV).

This passion-replacement therapy represents a whole recreation that has to be enacted by the Lord of creation. Bound by our passions, you and I cannot make ourselves feel other than what we feel any more than we can make ourselves love other than what we love or loathe other than what we loathe. We cannot re-create ourselves; rather, we must be recreated by the grace of our Lord, Christ Jesus.

Our redeeming Savior, out of his great love for us, made the choice to free us from our slavery to our passions. On the cross, Christ Jesus surrendered himself to our ungodly passions so that we could gain freedom from them.

When we make that journey to the cross and see there the One who suffered because of our passions, we experience ourselves being stripped of our prideful defenses. Our ungodly passions are left exposed, and we can no longer hide from ourselves who we are or what we have become. It is then that we can be washed clean (1 Corinthians 6:11) by God's forgiveness and set free.

Having washed us, our redeeming Savior then dwells with us— nurturing his passions in us—and we are recreated. "There is a new creation: everything old has passed away; see, everything has become new!" (2 Corinthians 5:17). We are, indeed, in debt to the One who came into this world bound in swaddling clothes. He chose to be subject to our passions; and with forgiving grace redeemed us from them at a cost, planting instead his passions in us. Our Savior is truly a redeeming Savior!

How would you describe your struggle with ungodly passions?

How would you describe the work of the redeeming Savior in your life?

What ungodly passions can the Advent/Christmas season stir in you?

What passions of Christ Jesus are being stirred up in you this Advent/Christmas season?

AN INVITING SAVIOR
LUKE 2:1-20

"And she gave birth to her firstborn son and wrapped him in bands of cloth, and laid him in a manger, because there was no place for them in the inn" (Luke 2:7).

We do not know the words with which the innkeeper turned away the tired couple that had traveled so far. The words may have been said rudely or said with sad understanding. Perhaps there was nothing the innkeeper could have done to help. Perhaps, with a little effort and imagination, a way could have been found to make room for the mother about to have a baby. However, no matter what words were used to turn away the exhausted family, the news was not inviting to the One soon to be bound in swaddling clothes and laid in a manger.

It is not just innkeepers in Bethlehem that seem to be lacking in hospitality when it comes to receiving the Lord of all creation. God finds the whole world, even God's own people, not inviting. "He was in the world, and though the world was made through him, the world did not recognize him. He came to that which was his own, but his own did not receive him" (John 1:10-11, NIV).

It is worth our while to meditate on this important difference between God and us. As the one bound in swaddling clothes, God chose to come into this "non-inviting" world so that God could invite us into God's world, the kingdom of God. Whether we choose to invite our Lord into this world or not, we still have an inviting Savior.

Given the inviting nature of our God, it is not surprising to find God present at this first Christmas, handing out invitations to a birthday party. It appears God is not selective about who God invites either. God even chose to send an invitation to a bunch of shepherds.

Shepherds were a rather suspect lot in the days of the first Christmas. The reputation of shepherds was so poor that rabbis warned parents not to let their children grow up to be shepherds. The word of a shepherd was considered to be so worthless that the testimony of shepherds was barred from court. To do business with a shepherd risked being associated with the criminal element of society, and a conscientious Pharisee would not take that risk. No respectable person would ever invite shepherds to a birthday party, but an inviting God did! Even shepherds are invited to that holy birthplace where God was encountered, face to face, as a Babe in a manger.

Having been raised in a churchgoing family, I have participated in my fair share of children's Christmas pageants. I have experienced the tension of wondering what role I would play while hoping to be chosen for the premier position of Joseph. Failing that role designation, I hoped to land the role of one of the three kings. I never did. I always ended up in that remaining bunch of boys to whom the director pointed and said, "I guess you boys can be shepherds."

Like many of us men, if it were not for shepherds being mentioned in Luke, I never would have gotten a part to play in the Christmas story. I now graciously see the truth of this observation: If God did not invite people such as the shepherds to come to that holy place in the presence of the One bound in swaddling clothes, a person like me would never have been offered a place in the great story of salvation.

I give thanks to an inviting Savior who still calls people like me into that holy place where I can meet the God of my salvation and come into the kingdom. God invites each of us to come to those hidden places where Christ dwells, meet the Savior there, and step into the Kingdom as we follow him.

I receive a lot of invitations in the mail, but most of them are invitations to buy products I do not need or to enter promotional contests on which I do not want to waste time. Sorting through the stack of mail before me, I will sometimes notice a small, hand-addressed envelop with my name on it and will know that it is an invitation to an event that is important to a friend or a loved one. I recognize it as an invitation to be opened, not one to be left unopened and thrown in a trash bin.

How do we recognize an invitation that comes from God? The shepherds were busy about their normal work, expecting the normal fare of a normal day. Because they were not waiting with anticipation for an invitation from God, God graciously gave them an invitation in a form difficult to miss— or dismiss. God's invitation to them included a choir of angels and a spectacular light show.

Why can't we get obvious invitations like that from God? I do not know the answer to that question, but I am convinced that an inviting God sends plenty of invitations to each of us in a form or style to which we can respond. For some of us, the sudden appearing of a choir of angels would engender more questions or fear than anything else. Had we been those shepherds, we might still be wondering if we really saw and heard the angels. Or perhaps we would have just stood there arguing if the angels we had just seen were Democrats or Republicans.

The season of Advent reminds us that with an inviting Savior dwelling in this world, we had best be on alert, watching for invitations that God sends. They may come in the form of a heart's sensation, in a sermon that pricks our conscience, in a sudden thought that turns to eternity, in a movement of compassion for another, in an opportunity for ministry, or in countless other ways.

While we must be watchful so that we do not miss God's invitations, we must also be sure that we act on the invitations we receive. After the shepherds received the invitation, they stopped what they were doing and went to the party. They had other options.

The shepherds could have bowed to a lesser boss and delayed their venture until after their watch was done; or they could have waited there in the field to see if God would send another invitation.

Instead, the shepherds went to "see this thing that has taken place, which the Lord has made known to us" (Luke 2:15). Because the shepherds acted on the invitation and arrived at the manger, Mary and Joseph had their trust in God confirmed by the shepherds report. In addition, the shepherds themselves found their trust in God confirmed by what they saw.

Some of us will never grow certain of God because we keep refusing to go to the places where God tells us we will meet God. If we do not act on God's invitation, we will never discover Christ is real nor will we ever truly follow Christ into the Kingdom.

The whole Advent and Christmas celebration is like one great angel chorus and light show for us. Some are transfixed by all the activity and are content to stay watching the sights and enjoying the sensations of Christmas. What must be remembered, however, is that behind all the celebration of the season there is an invitation that must be noticed, opened with great attention, and acted on. We must each make our way to the One bound in swaddling clothes and there take our step into the Kingdom by following him. The real action is not in the invitation; it is in the Kingdom as we follow Christ.

How have you experienced God's invitation to come and see Jesus this Advent and Christmas season?

How are you responding to the invitation you have received from God?

---

[1] From *The Interpreter's Bible*, Volume XI (Abingdon Press, 1955); page 531.
[2] From *The Interpreter's Bible*, Volume XI; page 531.